VIKING
MOBILE MARKETING

Chapter 1:
Why Mobile?

Hello and welcome to Viking Mobile Marketing. Here's a quick overview of what we'll be covering in this course:

First, we'll discuss why mobile marketing is so important to your business, no matter what industry you're in. Next, we'll go over how to make your sites and pages mobile friendly. After that, we'll take a look at the various methods of sending mobile traffic to your web properties. Finally, we'll cover a couple ways you can make special use of that mobile traffic when it shows up.

So without further ado, let's dive right in.

Why You Need Mobile Marketing

Mobile usage now represents 65% of all digital media time. As of 2016 mobile traffic makes up over 56% of all internet traffic to leading US websites. In response to this, 68% of businesses now have a mobile marketing strategy and by 2019, mobile advertising will represent 72% of all US digital ad spending.

But it's not just businesses that are catching on. Consumers are starting to expect more too. According to Google, 61% of users probably won't return to a mobile site they had trouble with and 40% of them will go to your competitors. 83% of consumers say a seamless experience on all their devices is very important while 57% insist they won't recommend businesses with a poorly designed mobile site. Of course, all that assumes users will even find a non-mobile-friendly site, which is becoming less likely now that google factors mobile-friendliness into your search ranking!

And that's all just pertaining to websites. Email mobile trends are even more eye-opening. Roughly 80% of consumers read their emails on a mobile device and a shocking 70% say they delete emails immediately if they don't look good on a mobile device! This means you need to be thinking mobile in your web design, your SEO, AND your email marketing. Otherwise, your business could suffer just like many others have who failed to jump on this mobile trend...

Luckily, you won't have that problem, because YOU found this awesome guide on mobile marketing. In the next few modules we're going to show you how to take this mobile trend by the horns and leverage it to your advantage. And it all starts by making sure your web properties are mobile friendly, which is what we'll discuss in the next module.

Chapter 2: Getting Mobile Friendly

The mobile marketing journey starts with making sure your web properties are mobile friendly. This is important for a few reasons. Firstly, it provides a positive and enjoyable experience for your visitors and customers, making them more likely to return to your site and more likely to speak and think highly of your business. Secondly, it caters to the fact that pretty soon a majority of your visitors will in fact be on mobile devices, if they aren't already. Thirdly, it will help you get found on search engines. Google has made it clear on multiple occasions that it seriously factors mobile friendliness into the search rankings and if you aren't mobile friendly, this means you'll be missing out big time on traffic.

So generally there are two ways to make a site "mobile friendly". The first is to create a separate mobile version of your site and the second is to make your existing site or page "mobile responsive". We'll look at each of these.

Mobile Versions

So until recently the first option, having a separate mobile version of your site or pages, was more common. Companies were either hiring people to build a separate mobile site from scratch on one hand or, on the other hand, they'd rely on certain site builders or content management systems (CMS) that would conveniently auto-generate and update a mobile version in real time when things were added to their desktop version. For most independent internet entrepreneurs, it was the latter option, of course. For example, on your desktop site you could add a headline to your homepage, and then a button, and then a cool background photo, and then a new navigation option to a new page and "poof" the mobile version of your site would immediately have an easily visible version of that headline, an easily tappable version of that button, and in the case of the photo, it would either shrink it and place it above or below your other elements, rather than as a background, or it would leave it as a background (but it wouldn't really look right on a vertically held device), or simply hide the image on the mobile version. As for the navigation option that was added, it would be added to a special mobile dropdown menu. Examples of the website builders or CMS's that did this (and maybe still do) are Weebly, Wix, and many others.

Problems with Mobile Versions

So it basically worked out okay. But there were a few problems. In many cases, not all the functionality would be available on the mobile version of the site. Entire buttons, options, and elements would be missing either because the designers wanted to keep things minimalistic or because the mobile web building platform they used didn't allow certain things. Many users didn't like this and made a habit of going straight to the bottom of any mobile page they found and looking for a "desktop version" link so they could simply enjoy the desktop version by pinching and zooming on their device.

The other problem, from a designer perspective, was that it was difficult to fully translate the business' brand image and feel and the full force of the desktop website presentation (like that stunning background image) onto these clunky, bulky, narrow mobile versions. Also, there were some problems with handling the ever increasing number of mobile devices, from phones to tablets, with varying screen sizes. For example, you had people on full tablets getting stuck on weird, stretched out mobile versions of sites on one hand and people with mini tablets might find themselves on the full desktop version of some sites. Adding the proper scripts to properly identify incoming traffic devices and redirect them to the appropriate version of the site simply became a pain in the neck, and this was complicated even more by the fact that many users had different preferences. Maybe the mini tablet owner did in fact prefer to pinch and zoom on desktop versions. Maybe the elderly full tablet user who didn't always have his or her reading glasses handy preferred the larger, bulky, minimalist layout of the mobile site stretched to fit the full tablet's biggish screen.

Point is, there was no way to make everybody happy and few options for flexible, multi-device friendliness. Then, along came responsive web design…

Responsive Sites

So the question was this: rather than have two versions of a site and struggle to please the vast numbers of new screen sizes and devices.... What if you could have just one version of your site that could then magically shrink and adjust in direct response to the size of the screen that it was being viewed on?

The industry produced what were called "responsive sites" and they immediately caught on. Depending on what type of CMS you use today, the mobile responsiveness might vary.

An ideal responsive site will do the following: Headlines, paragraphs, and text in general will have their font size and layout adjusted to look perfect on any screen and fill it from left to right. Background images, depending on the setting chosen such as center vs stretch, will adjust themselves appropriately to be reasonably visible on all devices. Image elements will shrink to fill the screen from left to right. Other elements like buttons or product images that may be arranged in a left to right, multi-row matrix or grid on a desktop site, are rearranged to be stacked on top of each other. For example, if you have 12 product images, each with a buy button below it, arranged in 3 rows of 4 images, then on a mini-tablet those rows might be adjusted to 6 rows of 2 images and on a smartphone they might become a single column of one stacked on top of the other while keeping their original left to right sequence/order and keeping the respective buy button under each image. And all of this happened automatically on the same site with no effort required on the website owner's part.

Get the picture? Now you see why responsive caught on so quickly, right? Now, responsive design isn't without its own cons and kinks and some businesses still find that the separate mobile site model still works better, so definitely sit down and determine which route is best for your business. Bottom line, look at the various options out there and come up with a plan to get your websites and landing pages mobile friendly ASAP.

Chapter 3:
Mobile Traffic

So once you've got your sites and pages mobile-friendly, you need to get some traffic to them. Depending on the purpose of your landing pages, you might be looking for mobile-only traffic or you might be looking at indiscriminate traffic in general and simply wanting to ensure that traffic is treated appropriately based on the visitors' devices.

In many cases, if you're goal is something mobile specific, like collecting people's primary, best email addresses and real names via a mobile opt-in tool like Warlord Mobile Leads, then you'll literally want ONLY mobile traffic coming to your landing pages.

We'll focus on free and paid methods of driving exclusively mobile traffic first, then indiscriminate traffic methods.

Mobile-Only Traffic

So let's say you're trying to collect super high quality email leads because you're tired of low open rates, fake email addresses, and all that jazz. In that case you'd need a tool like Warlord Mobile Leads to collect primary emails and real names without visitors needing to type any info into an opt-in form. Problem is, tools like that only work on mobile devices, so you don't really want to send desktop traffic to a page where you're using a tool like that. Likewise, perhaps you're trying to branch out into SMS text message marketing and you want users who see an SMS sign-up offer to be on their mobile devices when they see it. Point is, sometimes you're going to want exclusively mobile traffic. There's a couple ways to do this.

Firstly, you can use paid ads that run only on mobile. The high end version of this would be paid native ads on social media platforms like Facebook or Twitter. These ads, while slightly more expensive, can actually be the most cost-effective because of the quality of traffic they send. We won't go into great detail on how to create these ads since that's not the focus of this guide, but feel free to check out our other guides on Facebook and Twitter paid ads for more details. Suffice it to say, there is a very clear option in the creation process for these ads where you can choose to display the ad for mobile users only. Choose that option and all your traffic will be mobile.

Another paid option is to use mobile-specific ad networks like BuzzCity or Admoda. These platforms let you target mobile users who are browsing on mobile sites or using mobile apps within these platforms' respective networks. Remember those annoying text ads that you see while using the lite version of your favorite phone app? Yup, that's what we're talking about here. The benefit of this is that you can get your ad in front of a TON of people and the clicks are very inexpensive (as little as $0.01). The problem is that the traffic is much lower quality and less targetable. For example, if you're using native social media ads, like Facebook, you can market your heart health related products to men, over 50, in Texas, who have expressed interest in the American Heart Association or a certain brand of heart medicine. Bingo. But if that's your target market and you're using one of these super cheap mobile ad networks like BuzzCity, then you won't see much success. These networks do have some targeting capabilities but they're not nearly as specific or reliable as the major social media sites so you should only use them if your target audience is relatively broad to begin with.

Another newer option is Facebook Instant Articles. So Facebook instant articles is basically a big push by Facebook to create articles that show up in the Facebook Mobile App newsfeed and render in the blink of an eye without people having to be directed to an external page or wait for the article to load. The great thing about this is that it doesn't cost money and you guarantee that only mobile users will see these articles. So the idea is add these articles to your content marketing plan and ensure they link/lead to a mobile landing page. This is a solid non-paid method for driving mobile-only traffic.

Non-Discriminate Traffic

As for non-discriminate traffic, it's pretty simple. Just about every CMS will automatically show people the correct version of your site these days. Otherwise you can use a simple mobile redirect script or plugin to redirect mobile traffic away from a certain URL and over to your desired mobile landing page. Of course, if your site is responsive you don't even need to worry about this.

Chapter 4:
Making Use of
Mobile Traffic

After you've got some mobile traffic coming your way, you might be inclined to make specific use of it. The first use of mobile traffic is more or less passive. Namely, you get a good SEO boost from having a mobile site which has mobile traffic coming to it and staying on it because they enjoy it (rather than bouncing away within seconds because it's not mobile-friendly, which hurts your SEO). The second use of having mobile traffic coming to a mobile-friendly page is simply a positive brand image. Having an attractive mobile site reflects well on your business, makes people more likely to return and makes them more likely to speak highly of and share your business. This of course results in other things like mobile users clicking on your phone number to call your business or finding your opt-in forms or order buttons.

But there's another, much more practical and specific way to make use of mobile traffic that hardly anyone talks about. You see, it can be advantageous knowing what device people are on when they view your properties because of the different ways you can leverage those devices. Did you know that if a person's mobile device is prompted to send or prepare an outgoing email, by default that email will come from whichever email account they designated as their primary email in their phone settings? This is a mobile-specific concept.

Well, if you have mobile traffic, you can use a tool like Warlord Mobile Leads to actually create little opt-in buttons that, when tapped, create a prefilled outgoing email with your choice of subject and body text (e.g. "please send me the free report") and, when the user hits "send" that email is added to your email marketing/autoresponder mailing list along with their real name.

I'll give you a moment to rub your eyes and make sure you just read that correctly.

Yes, this means you can leverage mobile traffic to ensure your opt-ins and leads are actually people's real, primary email addresses and real names. This means your marketing emails end up in an inbox that is actually checked several times per day and you can personalize subject lines with people's names. This personalization has been shown to increase open rates by 29% and increase email campaign profitability by 73% while the overall effect of collecting primary email addresses and real names together via Warlord Mobile Leads has been shown to increase open rates by a whopping 533%! (no, that's not a typo).

Now, email marketing and high quality list building are not the focus of this particular guide, so we'll stop there. But the point is, if you're going to get mobile traffic, you might as well find a way to specifically leverage it.

Battle Plan

So here's your battle plan:

Step 1: Pick a CMS (or use your current one) and ensure your site and pages look great on mobile.

Step 2: Choose one or more methods for driving mobile traffic to your properties. We suggest you spend a small amount of money experimenting with a few different paid ad options.

Step 3: Leverage that traffic by using mobile-specific tools like Warlord Mobile Leads to build a high quality, high open rate email marketing list.

Don't wait. Take action and start executing this plan today!

www.ingramcontent.com/pod-product-compliance
Lightning Source LLC
Chambersburg PA
CBHW040931210326
41597CB00030B/5269